How To Backpack

Karl McCullough

How To Backpack
by Karl McCullough

ISBN 978-1-926917-19-1

Printed in the United States of America

Copyright © 2010 Psylon Press

All rights reserved. Except for use in a review, no portion of this book may be reproduced in any form without the express written permission of the author. For information regarding permission, write to admin@psylonpress.com

Neither the author nor the publisher assumes any responsibility for the use or misuse of information contained in this book.

Other books by Psylon Press:

100% Blonde Jokes
R. Cristi
ISBN 978-0-9866004-1-8

Choosing a Dog Breed Guide
Eric Nolah
ISBN 978-0-9866004-5-6

Best Pictures Of Paris
Christian Radulescu
ISBN 978-0-9866004-8-7

Best Gift Ideas For Women
Taylor Timms
ISBN 978-0-9866004-4-9

Top Bikini Pictures
Taylor Timms
ISBN 978-0-9866426-3-0

Cross Tattoos
Johnny Karp
ISBN 978-0-9866426-4-7

Beautiful Breasts Pictures
Taylor Timms
ISBN 978-1-926917-01-6

For more books please visit:
www.psylonpress.com

TABLE OF CONTENTS

Introduction	7
Chapter 1	9
Beginning backpacking	10
Selecting your first backpacking trip	10
How far?	11
Backpacking safely	14
Chapter 2	15
Backpacking equipment and gear	16
Backpack	16
Internal and external framed backpacks	18
Carrying capacity	19
Sleeping bag	19
Hiking boots	20
Choosing a tent	22
Sleeping pads	25
Waist pack	25
Travelers checks	25
Personal essentials	26
Toiletries	26
Miscellaneous	26
Clothing and shoes	26
Chapter 3	29
Safety matters	30
Packing a first aid kit	30
Understanding your physical condition	32
Anticipating the level of difficulty	33
Preventing lift injuries	34

Chapter 4	**35**
Planning your trip	36
Chapter 5	**41**
Planning international backpacking trips	42
Passports	42
Travel visas	44
Vaccinations	47
A few words about malaria	50
Dengue fever	51
Bird flu	51
Other health matters	51
Chapter 6	**53**
Transportation and accommodation matters	54
Budget airlines	56
Traveling by train	58
Hostels	58
Advantages of hostels	59
Disadvantages of hostels	60
Hostel etiquette	61
Travel Insurance	63
Chapter 7	**65**
Leaving for your trip	66
Backpacking checklist	67
3 Season backpacking checklist	70
Winter checklist	72
Food and meals	72
Breakfast foods	73
Lunch	73

Dinner	74
Backpacking recipes	74

Conclusion 77

Introduction

Backpacking is a hobby that is enjoyed around the world in a wide variety of different manners. From casual backpackers who hit the trails on the weekends to those adventurous souls who plan months in advance to spend a year or more backpacking their way through entire continents, backpacking is a passion for many.

For those not familiar with the idea of backpacking, it is much like hiking combined with camping with the exception that everything one needs for camping must be condensed and carried in a pack while navigating the trails of the area you are exploring.

Backpacking presents a number of advantages, which is why so many people have fallen in love with it. One of the primary advantages of backpacking is that it offers an inexpensive and easily affordable way of exploring a new area. Many people are drawn to the idea of backpacking because it makes it possible to get in touch with nature in a way that simply is not possible when traveling in any other manner. Still yet, others like the idea of backpacking because of the quality time that it allows them to spend with friends and family.

When you are out backpacking, there are usually no cell phones to worry about and certainly televisions or game stations claiming your attention. You are able to enjoy good conversation, the stillness of the night, the beauty of nature surrounding you and the excitement of discovering new wildlife, flora and fauna. Others are excited at the idea of being able to conquer the challenges that invariable come with backpacking.

While backpacking you will gain the opportunity to see places and things that otherwise would not be possible and which most people will only ever be able to read about or see on a television program. Perhaps even better, backpacking presents a wonderful way to exercise and stay in shape.

If the idea of backpacking sounds interesting and intriguing, you are about to start on a journey that many people come to love so much they try to hit the trails as often as possible. In this guide, we will examine some of the basics you should be aware of when getting started with backpacking, including some of the equipment you will need, some basic safety tips and information to help guide you whether you are planning a simple weekend backpacking trip or you are planning to backpack your way through Europe.

Let's get started!

Chapter 1

Beginning Backpacking

Okay, so you have decided to take a backpacking trip! What do you need to know before you get started? That is what we will examine in this chapter. When you are first getting started with the idea of backpacking it can be easy to become overwhelmed trying to figure out what kinds of equipment you must have, where you should go, how far to hike and how many days you should plan to spend on your backpacking trip.

Selecting your First Backpacking Trip

Before you do anything else, it is important to give some thought to where you will take your first trip. This is important because it will help to guide many other decisions, including how long you plan to spend on the trip and even the types of equipment that you will need. Most people find when they are getting started with backpacking that it is a good idea to start out small. While the idea of backpacking your way through Europe or the Australian outback may appeal to you, the simple fact is that if you are new to backpacking you will be better off if you start out small.

A great way to approach backpacking is to consider taking a trip in a national or state park. Many such parks have an excellent array of trails that are 12 miles or less and are ideal for beginning backpackers. Focus on choosing a trail that forms a loop so that you will end your trip where you started. If you choose a linear trail instead of a loop you will be forced to either pre-arrange to have a ride waiting for you at the end of your trip or back track to make it back to your vehicle. If you backpack with a partner you can take two vehicles for a linear trail, allowing you to easily leave a vehicle at each end of the trail.

You should also consider the terrain when you are choosing a trail. Remember that a six mile hiking trail that has a number of steep ascents and descents will naturally be far more difficult than a flat trail that is actually longer in distance. Look for a trail that has been well blazed and established as well. This is particularly important if you are just starting with backpacking. Even trails that are well established can sometimes be difficult to follow because of side trails.

How Far?

When determining how far you should go on your first trips it is extremely important to know your pace and keep it in mind. For your first trip, it is usually a good idea to plan a hike that will allow you to cover a reasonable distance overnight. Smaller trips will present you with the opportunity to learn about your equipment as well as your own abilities. During smaller trips you can also take advantage of the opportunity to learn more about your pace, which you can then utilize when you plan a longer trip.

You may find it helpful to take notes and record when you start and when you finish a hike as well as the distance you have traveled. This information can then be used to calculate your average pace and for calculating distance for future hikes. For instance, if you discover that your average pace is 1 ½ miles per hour then you will know that if you want to travel 15 miles per day on your next trip you should plan a minimum of 10 hours for your hike. Understanding this and adding in time for breaks will allow you to estimate when you need to hit the trails to reach your destination at a particular time. Of course, remember that you always need to take into consideration the differences that can exist on terrain between various trails.

Taking smaller trips is an excellent way to determine your own physical limitations before you attempt a trip that is longer in terms of distance as well as time. You may find that you are only able to hike comfortably for 4 or 5 hours before you must break for camp. Always remember that even when you do stop to make camp you will still have quite a bit to do, including pitching your tent, gather water, cooking and then cleaning up. If you take the time when you are first starting out to learn your limitations you will find that your trips will be far more comfortable and enjoyable. Ultimately, backpacking should not be about how many miles you can cover within a certain period of time, but enjoying the experience.

Once you have given some thought to how far you will initially travel for your first backpacking trip, you will then need to give some thought to a few other details. Begin by choosing a date for your trip. Go ahead and mark it down on your calendar.

Select a specific trail within the geographical location that you want to hike. Be aware that if you are hiking in a national or state park, there are likely to be numerous trails, so take the time to find out as much as possible about each option and then select a specific trail based on the distance and time that you would like to hike for your trip. Remember that some trails are either closed or inaccessible during certain times of the year. Other questions you should consider when choosing a trail include:

- Where will I leave my vehicle?
- How much water is available along this trail?
- Where are ideal campsites located on this trail?
- Will I need to register?
- Is there a fee for using this trail?

You can usually find the answers to these questions by researching the trail on the Internet or contacting the park office. Along with the questions listed above, you also need to make sure you are aware of any local fire regulations and hunting seasons that may be in effect.

Backpacking Safely

Backpacking can certainly be a wonderful experience, but in order to enjoy that experience as much as possible it is always important to keep safety considerations in mind.

First, remember that it is always safest to backpack with a partner. If something should happen while you are out on the trails, having a partner with you will make it possible for someone to either provide assistance or go for help. Do not make the mistake of thinking that you can rely on your cell phone for help while you are out on the trail. In many areas where you will be hiking, you will not be able to receive a signal on your cell.

Regardless of how far you plan to travel or how long you plan to be gone on your trip, always make sure that you let someone know where you plan to hike and when you plan to return. If you fail to show at the appointed time, at least someone will know there is a problem and be able to send a search and rescue crew.

Although we will go into this in more detail in the next chapter, keep in mind that it is always important to make sure that you have a first aid kit with you anytime you plan to be on the trail, even if you are only taking a short trip. Emergencies can occur even on short trips and it is always best to make sure you are prepared in advance.

Chapter 2

Backpacking Equipment and Gear

One of the most important elements of planning a backpacking trip is making sure that you have all of the correct equipment that you will need. When deciding what you will need for your backpacking trip there are a few areas that will need to be first taken into consideration. For example, you should consider how you will be backpacking and where you will be backpacking. If you decide to take a trip backpacking through a national or state park then you are likely going to need more equipment and gear than you will need if you backpack through Europe and plan to stay in hostels along the way. The climate and the time of year when you plan to take your trip can also play a role in the equipment and gear that you will need.

Backpack

At the top of your list, regardless of what type of trip you plan to take, should be a backpack. There are many different types of backpacks available on the market today and the exact type of backpack that you choose may depend upon how long you plan to be gone and how much equipment you plan to take with you.

Choosing a backpack is an extremely important matter. You will need to carry most if not all of your gear in your backpack so it needs to be spacious enough, but at the same time you need to make sure that it fits you appropriately your will be forced to deal with aches and pains as well as blisters during your trip.

The best way to find a backpack that will fit you correctly is to visit an outdoors or sporting goods store that specializes in selling backpacks and then try on backpacks with full weight. If you are new to backpacking you may not have a clear idea of what full weight is, but you should start out with at least twenty to twenty-five pounds. Walk around the store and pay attention to your body. The backpack should not rub or place too much pressure anywhere on your body. It also should not be constricting. The right backpack should feel comfortable.

Take your time and try on several backpacks until you find the one that feels best for you. Some stores will even allow you to rent gear so that you can actually test it out before you buy it.

Internal and External Framed Backpacks

One decision you may need to make when buying a backpack is whether to go with an internal framed or external framed backpack. An external framed backpack does present some advantages, including a variety of openings and pockets where you can access your gear. You will usually find that the majority of internal framed backpacks simply do not have as many access points and pockets as external framed backpacks.

In addition, external backpacks are often favored simply because of the frame. You can easily carry a sleeping back on the bottom of the frame and a tent on top, leaving the inside of the backpack for other gear and supplies. Furthermore, an external backpack is also much easier to hang on a post or a tree when you are out, which makes it easier to work with and find what you need.

Despite these advantages, internal framed backpacks remain quite popular and you will likely discover that there are more to choose from, including some that are fairly high tech. An internal framed backpack does present the advantage of riding closer to the body and being more form-fitting, which makes it easier to carry a sizeable load.

Carrying Capacity

Another consideration that will need to be made is the carrying capacity. It is essential that you choose a backpack that is sizeable enough for your needs. If you are going to only be taking overnight or weekend trips then a 3000 cubic inch pack will probably suffice for your needs. For longer trips, up to a week in duration, you should consider a 4000 or 5000 cubic inch pack.

If you plan to take extended trips, you should have a 5000 cubic inch pack at a minimum in order to make sure that you have enough space inside the pack to accommodate everything you will need for a lengthy trip.

Sleeping Bag

Beyond your backpack, the next most important piece of equipment on your list should be your sleeping back. There is perhaps nothing worse than not being able to sleep because you are not warm enough. It can make for a very unpleasant trip, which is why you should exercise great care in choosing a backpack that will keep you warm enough no matter where you happen to choose to travel.

There are two important factors to consider; temperature rating and size. Consider where you will be backpacking and the time of year. What are the typical lows at night for the geographical area where you will be traveling and for that time of year? Remember that it is always much easier to unzip the bag to cool off in warm weather than it is to try to get warm if the weather should turn cold and you are not prepared.

You also need to take into consideration the girth and length of the bag. If you happen to be tall you will need to pay close attention to the size of the sleeping bag and may even need to purchase a custom sleeping bag to make sure that it fits you well.

Another important area to consider is what the sleeping bag is filled with. The two main options are down and synthetic. Synthetic sleeping bags tend to be heavier and bulkier but have the advantage of being less expensive. Also, synthetic sleeping bags perform better in wet weather than down sleeping bags.

Hiking Boots

The third most important piece of gear that you will take with you on your backpacking trips is your boots. Considering the amount of time that you will be on your feet, the shoes that you wear really are quite crucial. During your trip you will likely be hiking up as well as down hills and may even encounter some terrain that is rocky. Your feet will need to be protected not only from fatigue but also from the roughness of the trail and possible blisters.

When choosing the boots for your trip, there are several important factors to consider. First, you will want to make sure that you choose a boot that provides adequate support for your ankle. Today there are certainly many different types of options on the market, but if you are going to be doing any serious hiking you will do better to have a pair of sturdy boots rather than anything lightweight. The boots you wear can make a difference between a comfortable trip and hobbling home with a sprained ankle.

Waterproofing is also an essential element to consider. There is no doubt that at some point while you are out on the trail your shoes are going to get wet. That is just a given. There is not much worse than having to hike around in boots that are wet. Go the extra step and make sure that your boots are waterproofed and you will not regret it.

Of course, fit is also another important consideration. Ideally, it is best if you purchase your boots from a backpacking outfitter that is experienced in properly fitting boots. Your boots should fit your fit in a snug manner but should not be tight. If your boots are not snug fitting they will usually end up rubbing your feet and you will have blisters as a result. Your boots also should not slide forward so that your toes will rub into the top of the boot. This can be a problem if you are going downhill and if it happens you will likely end up with sore feet and more than one blister.

While trying on boots, make sure that you wear the same type of socks that you will be wearing while hiking to make sure that you get the right fit. Hiking or boot socks are typically thicker than the socks you would wear on a normal basis. They are usually made of either wool or synthetic. Cotton is usually not a good choice because it simply will not keep you warm during wet weather.

Once you have the right boots make sure you take the time to break them in before you actually hit the trail. If you try to skip over this step you will simply be asking for problems. The actual amount of time that you need to spend breaking in your boots will vary based on the type of boot and the material used. Softer boots can usually be broken in faster than boots made with a tougher material.

Keep in mind that while you are out on the trail, it is usually a good idea to remove your boots and socks from time to time and rub your feet. This will provide a nice break and give your boots an opportunity to air out some.

Choosing a Tent

You will also need a tent for your backpacking adventure, unless you know in advance that you plan to stay in hostels along the way. Even if that is your plan, keep in mind that sometimes things can happen that will interrupt your plans and it is always a good idea to be prepared just in case.

There are many different types, sizes, styles and shapes of backpacking tents. There are three main factors that you need to keep in mind when choosing a tent. They are weight, season and size. The most important element to focus on first is choosing a tent that will be appropriate for the season when you plan to be backpacking. Naturally, a tent that is suitable for taking a trip in the summer will not be appropriate for wintertime.

Size is also an important issue. Backpacking tents are not like camping tents, which may have three separate rooms. You must be able to carry your tent on your back, which means that it must be lighter and smaller than most tents. If you are backpacking, at the most you are probably only going to be able to carry a two-person tent, although there are some backpacking tents that are capable of accommodating up to three people.

Manufacturers understand that weight is an important issue so they strive to make backpacking tents as light as possible. The best way to do this is by using either less material or lighter material.

When choosing a tent, to make sure that it will fit all of your needs, it is a good idea to lay it out and imagine whether it will provide enough space for you to comfortably sleep inside with your sleeping bag. Do not forget to consider the shape and the height of the tent. The height that is listed is the height of the tent at its highest point. This can be an important consideration if you are tall because most tents will drastically slope from the highest point. You need to be sure that the tent you choose will be large enough for you to feel comfortable as well as store your equipment and gear. At the same time, you need to be sure that it is not so heavy that it will be a burden to carry while you are hiking during the day.

When it comes to being seasonally appropriate, you will find that most tents have either a 3 or 4 season rating. The difference lies in the strength of the material and the amount of ventilation that is offered. If you are backpacking during the winter, you are usually going to encounter some high winds as well as some possible snow, some of which will land on your tent. This means that your tent needs to be more durable. For winter, you will need a 4 season tent. If you are backpacking during any other time of the year, you are probably going to need some air circulation to account for the warmer temperatures.

Technically, a 4 season tent can be used during any time of the year and a 3 season tent can even be used in the winter, provided that the temperatures are not too extreme and you do not encounter a lot of snow.

Sleeping Pads

The purchase of a sleeping pad is another important consideration. While a sleeping pad will not necessarily made the ground any softer, it can provide some insulation from the damp and cold. There are many different options to choose from including foam pads, egg crate style foam, self-inflating, etc.

If you choose to go with a foam pad, it is a good idea to choose one that has a closed cell type construction to ensure that it will not absorb water if it rains and your tent leaks.

Waist Pack

Along with a backpack, you may find it helpful to bring along a waist pack in which you can keep items such as your wallet, maps, camera, etc. This can be particularly important if you are exploring a new city and prefer not to bring your entire backpack with you and would rather leave it a campsite or at a hostel while you are out and about.

Travelers Checks

Most people find that it is much easier to travel using travelers checks than with actual cash. $50 checks work well and will provide you with some peace of mind so that you do not have to worry about your wallet and cash or credit cards being stolen or lost during your trip.

Personal Essentials

Along with the items listed above you will also need to make sure that you bring along some essential personal items such as your driver license or identification, passport if traveling out of the country, camera and sunglasses.

Toiletries

You will naturally need some personal toiletries to use during your trip, such as a toothbrush, soap, toothpaste, shampoo, shaving items, a small towel, hairbrush or comb, toilet tissue, deodorant and aspirin or pain killers. A pair of waterproof sandals is also a good idea to bring along if you stay in a hostel or choose to use the public showers and rest rooms that are often available in park facilities.

Miscellaneous

Other items that you should make sure to bring with you include maps of the area(s) where you will be traveling and a book or some other reading material.

Clothing and Shoes

Naturally, you will also need to make plans to bring some clothing and shoes you but at the same time keep in mind that you need to pack and travel light. If you are traveling from state to state or abroad, it is a good idea to plan to bring one nice outfit just in case you decide to go to a nice restaurant. Otherwise you should plan to bring one or two pairs of pants, a couple of shirts, a sweatshirt or light jacket and a raincoat. When it comes to shoes, bring a pair of nice shoes and a pair of comfortable walking shoes.

Chapter 3

Safety Matters

In the first chapter we briefly discussed some safety guidelines, but in this chapter we are going to take a more in depth look at this topic, due to its importance. Backpacking can certainly be fun as well as challenging, but there is no getting around the fact that it can also be dangerous. It is not uncommon for injuries to occur on the trail, even if they are minor. It is possible to minimize the risk of injuries by planning ahead. Planning ahead and being well prepared can actually save your life when you are out on the trail.

Before leaving you should always make sure you know where you are going and how long you will be gone. Provide this information to a family member or a friend as well as solid information regarding the nearest contact point, such as a ranger station.

Packing a First Aid Kit

Bringing a first aid kit is essential to safety on the trail. You can easily purchase a kit at a camping our sporting goods store that will already be stocked or you can make your own, but be sure that your kit has all of the essentials that you will need, including the following:

Pain Killer

Ibuprofen or acetomenophen; whatever you prefer, but make sure that you have some with you, preferably in individual packets.

Allergy Medication

If you have seasonal allergies you will definitely want to make sure that you have some allergy medicine along for the trip, preferably non-drowsy.

Medicated Creams

You should also have a supply of various medicated creams, including hydrocortisone cream for insect bites and stings and medicated cream that can be applied to cuts and scrapes.

Bandages

Make sure you have a few different sizes that will work well for different injuries.

Other items to include:

- Alcohol prep pads
- Gauze pads
- A roll of first aid tape
- ACE bandage
- Small medical scissors
- Tweezers

- Hand sanitizer
- Snakebite kit
- First aid guide with guidelines for treating various injuries

Understanding your Physical Condition

It is also important to make sure that you understand your own physical condition before you hit the trail. Beyond simply knowing that you are in good shape, it is a good idea to schedule a checkup with your physician and be sure that everything checks out before you head out onto the trail. When you are out backpacking is certainly not the time to have a medical emergency.

When it comes to your physical condition, it is also really important to be certain that you are ready before you hit the trail. Individuals who already exercise on a regular basis will likely find that they are in good enough shape to tackle a backpacking trip over easy to moderate terrain. Just to be sure, you may find it helpful to go ahead and strap on your pack fully loaded and then take a walk around the neighborhood for a couple of miles and make sure that you still feel comfortable.

If you are new to the idea of backpacking, it is really a good idea to gradually work your way up to it. Take some short day hikes with your pack and then work on gradually increasing your levels of endurance and conditioning.

Remember that if you are not in shape and do not exercise regularly, it is critically important that you focus on that before attempting any kind of backpacking trip. There are many different ways to do this including biking, swimming, walking, etc. While machines are great, it is really best to focus on doing as much as you can yourself, especially walking, since that is what you are going to be doing the most of when you are out on the trail. Whatever you decide to do, make sure you stick with it and you are consistent and you will find that in no time at all you will be in shape and ready to plan your first backpacking trip.

Anticipating the Level of Difficulty

The importance of anticipating the level of difficulty for the specific trip you are planning cannot be stressed enough. Every trail is different and it is crucial that you anticipate how difficult that trail is going to be and how much gear you are going to need to carry with you. Make a point to plan several weeks in advance, at least, by carrying the anticipated load for your tip.

Preventing Lift Injuries

Depending upon how long you plan to be gone for your trip, you could easily need to carry between 25 and 50 pounds of equipment with you. That is quite a load to be swinging onto your back each and every day, so it is important to make sure that you do it safely to avoid a lift injury. Try placing your pack on the ground so that the shoulder harness is facing you. Now, grab the shoulder straps with one in each hand and then with your knees slightly bent, place your knee into the back padding of the pack and pull it up your leg to your upper thigh.

You can then use your leg under the pack for support and slide first one arm through the shoulder harness and then the other arm. Tighten the hip belt and secure the pack. You may also find it helpful to place your pack on a stump or some other object and then squat down so that you can slip into the shoulder harness.

Chapter 4

Planning your Trip

One thing to keep in mind regarding taking a backpacking trip is that nothing is ever really set in stone. It is more than likely that while you are out on the trail you will see something or meet someone along the way that will cause you to change your itinerary. With that said, you do need to start somewhere and you certainly need to have some idea of what to expect along the way.

The two most important things that you need to know when planning a backpacking trip is the country where you plan to start and when you would like to go. Most people will find that it is easier to start out in their own home country, but at some point you may very well want to explore another country so it is a good idea to understand some basics of backpacking through a foreign country as well.

Keep the following guidelines in mind when planning your trip.

Always account for seasonal weather. Many areas of the world that are tropical in nature may have months of continual rain. It can be difficult to enjoy yourself if you are backpacking through an area and it is constantly raining. The advantage is that there will likely be few other people there and prices for hostels and other accommodations will be extremely cheap.

Make sure you budget accordingly. You will find that you get far more for your money if you take the time to find out what to expect regarding prices before you head out for your trip. For the most part, backpacking through North America, Europe and Australia is going to be more expensive than other areas that are considered to still be developing such as South America or Southeast Asia.

Plan the timing for your trip carefully. Beyond weather considerations, you should also take into consideration large festivals and tourist seasons that are likely to be crowded. You do not want to miss the opportunity to enjoy cultural events and other activities that can really add to your experience, but at the same time you do not want your trip to be marred by the fact that there are large crowds and it is difficult to get around and find alternate accommodations either.

Consider the political climate if you are going to backpacking through another country. While the dangers of traveling to another country always appear to be played up by the media, the reality is that there are actually some places where you do not want to find yourself if things become tense politically. Take the time to stay on top of things and know what is going on.

Language considerations. This is probably one of the biggest stumbling blocks that deters many people from considering traveling to another country. You should never let a lack of knowledge of the local language hold you back from an experience of a lifetime. The truth of the matter is that English is spoken in a great majority of the world and you can usually get by. In addition, once you arrive you will be surprised at how quickly you pick up the local language.

After you have decided on the area where you plan to begin your trip, it is a good idea to pick up a guide book for that region. There are many excellent quality guidebooks on the market today that can provide you with in-depth information about where to visit while there, what to expect and even how to travel on a budget. Keep in mind that while such guidebooks can certainly be beneficial and enlightening, they are not the comprehensive guide for everything that you will encounter so be prepared to be flexible.

As previously mentioned, it is always safer and oftentimes more fun to travel with someone, but everyone is different and you might find that the idea of backpacking on your own is immeasurably better than trying to backpack with another person and having to accommodate their schedule, needs and desires. On one hand you might feel that you are more comfortable if you have a familiar face with you, while on the other hand you might discover that it is better to be able to meet new people along the way without the constraints and restrictions that a travel partner can sometimes impose.

Only you can really decide which option is best for you, but keep in mind that this is really an important decision, especially if you plan to be gone for an extended period of time. If you are not certain whether you would prefer to travel with a partner or on your own you may find it easier to take a short trip, even a weekend trip, first with your prospective travel partner and see how that goes before you plan a long and extensive trip. Remember that travel can sometimes be stressful and you never know how someone is going react, even someone you think you know extremely well, until you are actually on the trail with them. It is much better to plan for a weekend trip and find out whether you are compatible travel partners over the course of two days than to discover that you cannot stand the way the other person whines while you are halfway through a month long trek backpacking through Europe.

Ultimately, while it is certainly important to handle some planning for your trip in advance, remember that the best way to soak up the culture of any area and enjoy the experience of backpacking is to allow yourself to be a wanderer. Try not to regiment yourself to a set schedule too closely. Remain flexible, keep your eyes open for interesting opportunities and experience and simply go wherever the road may take you.

Chapter 5

Planning International Backpacking Trips

At some point in time you may find yourself desiring to backpack through another country. There are certainly many advantages to recommend it, including the fact that it is the least expensive way to experience another country and it is a great way to soak up the culture. There are a few things that you need to keep in mind regarding practical matters if you are going to plan a backpacking trip in another country; however.

Passports

If you are going to travel outside of your own country, you are going to need a passport. This is something that is non-negotiable and it can sometimes be a bit time consuming so it is much better to go ahead and begin arrangements to obtain a passport sooner rather than later. New requirements have been put into place for the purposes of homeland security, which means that it can take eight weeks and sometimes even longer to obtain a passport. If you must have your birth certificate re-issued then you should expect that it will take even longer to obtain a passport.

The most convenient way to obtain a passport is actually through your Post Office. To obtain a passport, you will need the following items:

- A passport form-completed
- Proof of US citizenship (birth certificate or other relevant document)
- Photo Identification (student ID, driver license, etc.)
- Two qualifying passport quality photos

There are many places that offer passport photos for a relatively small fee. Keep in mind that it can actually be hard to take a photo of yourself that is considered to be qualifying, so plan in advance to get it done correctly.

After you have your photo, you will need to have copies made. The extras can be handy to have for visa applications as well as for providing at border crossings.

Once you have been issued your passport, make sure that you take very good care of it. If you happen to lose your passport while you are traveling out of country, you will have more problems that you want to experience. If your passport becomes damaged, you are also running the risk that you may experience problems at border crossings and even the possibility that you will be denied entrance.

Keep in mind that American passports are extremely valuable on the black market. Make sure you keep your passport safe and do not leave it lying around or you may find yourself minus a passport.

Travel Visas

When traveling out of country you will also likely need visas for travel. Travel visas are special types of stickers or stamps that are meant to be placed inside your passport and which will allow you cross over into another country. Some countries do not require travel visas while others require that you have once in advance. The subject of travel visas can be so important that it is possible for you to be detained at an airport and placed back on the plane if you did not obtain the proper travel visa in advance.

The difficult part of dealing with travel visas is that requirements regarding visas can chance every year from country to country, so it is incredibly important to make sure that you obtain the most recent and reliable information. The best way to handle the matter is to contact the embassy in your destination and ask for the latest visa requirements regarding your country of citizenship. Different travel requirements can apply for different countries of origin, so do not make any assumptions.

There are some countries that offer what is known as 'visa on arrival.' This means that you will be able to obtain the visa that you need when you arrive at the border crossing or airport. Most of these visas have a length of 30 days but some may only be good for two weeks, so make sure that you check the date. In some instances it may be better to go ahead and obtain the visas you will need in your country of origin before you arrive at your destination. This can help you to avoid having to stand in a long line at the airport and may be able to allow you to stay a bit longer before the visa expires and you have to make your way back to the border.

You will typically need to mail your passport along with completed forms to the embassy of your destination in your home country in order to obtain visas for travel. The embassy will collect a fee, stamp your passport and then mail it back to you. If you do decide to go with this option, keep in mind that it is certainly worth it to pay the additional fee to have it sent certified mail and to have it tracked. Considering the difficulty that can be involved in obtaining a passport, this can give you some peace of mind.

It should be remembered as well that visa requirements in some countries can be quite different and can even be daunting. Many countries have a rule known as the 'onward ticket' requirement, meaning that you must be able to prove that you have a means for exiting the country before they will allow you to enter. Not all countries that have this rule actually enforce it but some do, so you should be prepared for that.

You also should be familiar with basic etiquette for borders. There is no getting around the fact that some border officials are easier to deal with than others. Like everyone else, border officials have bad days and when that happens it may not be as easy as you had hoped to cross the border and get on with your travels. The best thing that you can do is to make sure that you are as nice and polite as possible, even if you happen to run across an official that is not as polite. Make sure you pay attention to what they are asking and comply with their regulations.

You can expect to be asked several routine questions when you arrive at a border such as "What is your business here?" and "What is your occupation?" Focus on giving answers that are honest and short and you should have no problems. If you are not working at the time, just tell them you are a student, even if it means that you are a student of life.

Vaccinations

If you are going to be traveling out of country, one area that you will want to pay particular attention to is making sure that you have all of the appropriate vaccinations for the country where you will be traveling. Certainly no one likes to be jabbed with a needle and the cost can be even more of a burden, but many of the diseases that you can come into contact with while traveling out of country can be quite serious, if not deadly, so it is important to handle this before you leave.

In some instances you must be able to show proof of a certain vaccination or you will not even be allowed to obtain a visa to enter a country. This is particularly true in portions of Africa and South America. Always make sure that you keep excellent records regarding your vaccinations and you can save yourself a good deal of trouble. Fortunately, many immunizations will last for at least five years if not ten, so it is not something that you will have to concern yourself with too frequently.

In most cases you can obtain vaccinations at a local clinic, but make sure that you book your appointment well in advance because you may need to wait a period of time between one injection and receiving another; such as the case with hepatitis vaccinations. Do not wait until the last minute to take care of receiving your vaccinations or you may be forced to alter your travel plans.

Vaccinations for travel can sometimes be expensive, so you should be prepared for this in advance. Some of the more rare vaccinations can cost almost $100 per injection and you may need to have multiple injections to be fully covered. Depending upon your health insurance, some of your injections may be covered, but some may not. Be sure to call in advance and review your policy.

Obviously, the vaccinations that you might need will vary depending upon exactly where it is that you plan to travel, but there are some basic immunizations that you should have and which will protect you when traveling to several countries. They include:

Hepatitis A-this vaccine is a good one to have for almost any travel and is typically good for 10 years. You will usually need to injections.

Heptatitis B-Another good one to have, typically good for ten years, but usually requires three injections.

Tetanus-Typically good for ten years. Many people will have received this while they were in school, but if it has been more than ten years, you should have another.

If you plan to travel to a developing area such as South America or South East Asia, you should consider the following immunizations:

Japanese Encephalitis-this vaccination is to protect you from a type of brain swelling disease that is carried by mosquitoes. It is most commonly found in rural areas. It requires three shots and they are not pleasant but if you do plan to travel into the more rural areas, it is worth it.

Typhoid Fever-Fortunately, you can now take pills instead of having an injection. The pills are good for five years.

Yellow Fever-If you plan to travel to parts of Africa and South America you will need to have proof of this vaccination.

Remember that information regarding vaccinations can change so it is always important to research the most recent information ahead of time. You can do this by checking with the CDC.

You may find it to be helpful to take a folder with you on your trip where you can keep information regarding your vaccinations easily organized. You certainly do not want to lose the information and then have to deal with the expense, pain and hassle of having to have duplicate vaccinations.

A Few Words about Malaria

Malaria is a very serious disease. Estimates indicate that around the world it kills approximately two people every single minute. As many as nearly 3 million people die from it each year. This disease is carried by mosquitoes and is not discriminating about where it is prevalent geographically. There is no vaccination for malaria but you can take preventative tablets.

There are now a few different types of anti-malarial pills and your health clinic or doctor should be able to recommend the best type of pills based on where you will be traveling. The problem is that the mosquitoes in many areas that are well traveled have developed an immunity to certain malarial tablets, so it is important to be very specific when you are speaking to your doctor about where you plan to travel.

You should also be aware that anti-malarial tablets can create sun unpleasant side effects including stomach problems and nightmares. If you are a female and you take birth control, they can interfere with the effectiveness of your birth control. Always follow the advice of your doctor, but in most cases you should plan to take the pills a minimum of one week before you plan to leave to allow ample time to be sure that there are no reactions and that they will be effective before you enter an area that is infected.

Dengue Fever

This is a disease that is not fatal but fairly common. It is also carried by mosquitoes that are located in Central and South America, Australia, Southeast Asia and islands in the Pacific. While Dengue fever will not kill you, it also is not pleasant and it can certainly interfere with your travel plans. Like malaria, there is no vaccination for Dengue fever, but it is important to try to avoid mosquito bites whenever possible to reduce your chances of becoming infected.

Bird Flu

Many people are concerned about outbreaks of bird flu, but you should know that for the most part they are fairly rare. The best thing to do is to not handle any live birds and stay away from bird feces.

Other Health Matters

Beyond vaccinations, you may find it to be a good idea to have an overall checkup before you leave for your trip. This certainly is not required to obtain a travel visa but it can help to rule out any problems before you leave and ensure that you enjoy your trip as much as possible.

If you take any prescription medications, make sure that you have an ample supply before you leave for your trip. Maintain a copy of your prescription with your medication so that there will not be any questions when you need to come through customs. You should also make sure that you keep all of your pills in the original and labeled bottles.

Chapter 6

Transportation and Accommodation Matters

While a backpacking trip is typically spent on foot hiking from one destination to another, you may need to arrange some transportation in order to get you to your initial point of departure, especially if you are planning to backpack through another country.

If you are going to be flying to the area where you plan to start your backpacking trip, it can be helpful to know how to find the cheapest flights possible. One of the best ways to do this is to book your ticket in advance. The further in advance that you reserve your ticket the more money you will be able to save in most cases. Try to book at least three weeks if not more so in advance.

On the flip side of this, sometimes if you wait until the absolute last minute you may be able to purchase a ticket at a drastically reduced cost if the flight was not sold out. There is a risk associated with this; however, if you are set on leaving on that date because if the flight is mostly booked you may not be able to find a discounted seat and will actually have to pay more.

Whenever possible, try to avoid flying on the weekends. This is the most expensive time to fly. Instead, try to leave on a Monday, Tuesday or Wednesday. Traveling around holidays can also be incredibly expensive because there are so many people traveling, there is a greater demand.

If you are planning to purchase a round trip ticket, you should know that a ticket with a span of more 90 days will usually cost more. Instead of actually purchasing a round trip ticket, consider purchase two 1-way tickets. This will usually be cheaper and will give you more flexibility.

While morning flights are sometimes cheaper, try to be flexible about the time of day that you leave. A cheap ticket can be released at any time of the day, so stay flexible and you may be able to save some money.

Be sure to check the sizing of your luggage before you leave. If it is overweight or oversized, you will usually have to pay extra. Also some airlines are actually now charging for carry-on luggage.

Also, be aware that you may be able to save money if you book a flight with a longer layover. While it may not be as convenient, if you really need to save some money this is one way to do it.

Try to fly into the largest city possible when you are visiting out of country. You can then take an airline hop or simply travel overland from your point of arrival to reach your actual destination.

Some possible good online options for locating inexpensive flights include:

www.expedia.com

www.orbitz.com

www.cheapoair.com

www.travelocity.com

www.hotwire.com

www.cheaptickets.com

www.skyscanner.net

www.sidestep.com

Budget Airlines

One of the newest and least expensive ways to travel is by a budget airline. These are quite popular in Africa and Europe, allowing you to often obtain a cheap flight for less than what it what cost to travel by train or bus. Such cheap flights are usually made possible through government subsidizations.

If you consider using a budget airline, keep the following guidelines in mind:

- First, you always get what you pay for. If the flight is on a budget airline, you can expect longer lines and delays. If you are not in a hurry and you want to save money this may be an option for you, but be prepared in advance.

- There are typically no free beverages or meals served on budget flights so plan in advance and bring your own.

- The restrictions for luggage size and weight are often far more strict on budget flights.

- Make sure that you allow plenty of time for checking in. One of the ways that a budget flight saves money is by hiring few attendants and that means delays.

- Always check in advance to see if a route is going to be open when you want to travel. During low seasons, it is not uncommon for a route to be shutdown if there are not enough passengers.

Traveling by Train

At one time, the best way to get around Europe was by train. While they are not as popular as they once were, trains are still very much in use and they are a fun way to travel.

If you have not traveled by train in the past you should know that booking train tickets can be a bit more complicated than booking a flight, so do not leave it to the last minute. Some excellent resources for booking train travel include:

www.railpass.com

www.raileurope.com

www.railkey.com

Hostels

If you are going to be making your way through Europe one of the best and most popular ways to handle your accommodations is by staying in a hostel. This is a wonderfully inexpensive form of accommodation that will also give you the opportunity to meet many other people who are also traveling. The most important thing to keep in mind about hostels is that they are by nature a social setting. While most do offer private rooms, many also have dorms in which there are several beds. Most also provide self-catering kitchens and some even provide meals. You will find hostels in a variety of different settings so they do give you an opportunity to enjoy a number of experiences. In fact, you should not be surprised to find many hostels situated in some rather remarkable buildings, including castles. Most hostels are independently owned and operated. Some even have their own restaurants and bars.

The thing to keep in mind is that staying in a hostel is much different than staying in a hotel. There is much more openness in a hostel than in a hotel and if you are not the type of person who enjoys socializing, meeting new and different people and opening yourself up to new experiences, this may not be the best option for you.

Advantages of Hostels

There are some significant advantages associated with saying in a hostel, including:

- Location-hostels are often located in convenient locations, near public transportation and downtown areas

- Affordable-compared to a hotel, a hostel can be extremely affordable. If you sleep in a dorm as opposed to a private room, you can save quite a lot of money.

- Wide range of ages-when staying in a hostel you will find that you encounter plenty of young people but there are also likely to be senior citizens, middle-aged people and even families.

- Social interaction-another great advantage of staying in a hostel is the opportunity to meet and interact with people from around the world. Shared common areas and cooking facilities can help you to develop friendships that can really add to your travel experience.

- Relaxed atmosphere-hostels that are independently owned typically have an atmosphere that is very relaxed and warm. Most allow you to bring your own alcohol and there is typically no curfew imposed.

Disadvantages of Hostels

While there are many advantages to staying in a hostel, it is a different way of traveling and it is one that is not right for everyone. Some possible disadvantages include:

- Close proximity-many dorm rooms have ten bunks per room. If you are a private type person, this may be too close for your comfort

- Noise-hostels are often noisier than hotels and if you are person who enjoys peace and quiet, it is not likely to be your cup of tea

- Cleanliness-the simple fact is that with so many people in and out on a regular basis, it can be hard for things to be kept clean.

- Mix of ages-if you are an older traveler, you may not wish to stay in the same room with younger travelers, who are naturally noisier and more boisterous

- Shared bath facilities-just like the sleeping accommodations, you should understand that you will likely need to share bath accommodations.

- Not as much comfort and luxury-the key advantage to a hostel is the affordability and that means that there will not be as many luxuries or comforts as would be provided in a hotel.

Hostel Etiquette

If you do decide that a hostel is the right choice for you, there are a few matters of etiquette that you should be aware of which can make your trip more pleasant and enjoyable for you as well as for the others who may be staying there.

Be Quiet

While certainly no one expects other travelers to walk on eggshells the entire time they are there, after about 10 pm or so at night, it is always important to try to keep the noise down. Some people do like to turn in early and it is considerate for you to be quiet and allow them to do that. Of course, it's almost impossible to maintain complete silence in a dorm room but exercise some consideration and if you want to talk, take it outside.

Lights Off

In general, you should keep the lights off before sunrise and after 11pm. No one wants to be woken up by bright lights. If you need to move around, use a small flashlight.

Keep things Clean

Remember that a maid is not one of the amenities that comes with staying in a hostel. Pick up after yourself. When you are finished with your dishes, wash them and put them away.

Pack Early

It is always best to pack your bags the night before so that you do not have to do it early the next morning and run the risk of bothering others who may be trying to get a bit more sleep.

Travel Insurance

Travel insurance is not a necessity while you are backpacking, but it is certainly something that should be considered. For the most part, travel insurance is relatively inexpensive if you are going to be taking a backpacking trip. There are many good reasons to consider taking out backpacking travel insurance, including:

- Most such policies will cover your backpack if it is lost or stolen along with other items such as your camera

- Many policies will cover your trip if you should have to cancel it

- It can save you a lot of money if something should happen and you become ill or injured while you are traveling

If you do plan to purchase backpacking travel insurance, there are a few things to keep in mind. First, always make sure that you do your homework and that the company that you purchase coverage from will actually cover where you are going and what you are going to be doing, including any particular adventures you may want to take such as rock climbing, white water rafting, etc. Never assume. Ask.

Find out whether the policy allows for you to extend your coverage online if you should decide that you want to stay longer. This can be an extremely convenient feature.

Chapter 7

Leaving for your Trip

Okay, the time has finally arrived and now you are ready to leave for your first backpacking trip. The first thing that you need to do is make sure that you have all of your gear and equipment gathered. You do not want to leave anything behind. Check everything in advance and take care of any repairs that may be needed before you leave. Also, check all of your supplies and make sure that you replenish anything that may have been used previously such as matches, personal hygiene products, first aid kit supplies, etc.

Also, check the batteries for your flashlight, make sure you have spares and check your food supplies. Remember that it is much easier to check all of the items in advance and make sure that you have what you need before you leave than to get 50 miles down the trail and realize you forgot something.

Before leaving, always make sure that you check the weather forecast and that you have the clothing and gear that is appropriate for the weather you will be facing. If you are going to be hiking with others, confirm the date and the time of departure with your partners. If you are planning to share equipment and supplies with your partners, be sure you know in advance who is going to supply what.

One to two days before you plan to leave, conduct a final weather check and check once again to be sure that you have everything that you need for the upcoming trip.

Backpacking Checklist

- Backpack
- Compression straps or rope
- 1 Or 2 water bottles
- Metal / plastic bowl & cup
- Metal / plastic spoon
- Light weight sleeping bag
- Emergency blanket
- Sleeping pad
- 1 Or 2 changes of underwear
- Optional change of shorts
- Rain jacket or poncho
- Compass
- First aid kit
- Flashlight & spare batteries
- Pocket knife
- Trash bags
- Gallon freezer zip plastic bags
- Tooth brush & tooth paste
- Foot powder
- Wash cloth, small towel & very small bar of soap
- Bug repellent
- Sun screen
- Hat
- 2 - Large handkerchief or bandannas
- Rope or nylon twine
- Water proof matches
- 2 Or 3 clothespins

- Backpacking saw
- Cat hole shovel & tissue paper
- Cook pot
- Water purifier
- Backpacking stoves & fuel
- Collapsible water containers
- Camp suds & bleach
- Plastic dish scrubber
- Ground cloth
- Sleeping pad

Food & Drink
- Water filter or tablets
- Cup
- Plastic plate or bowl
- Silverware/flatware
- Swiss army knife
- Non perishable food
- Seasoning/spices
- Cooking pots
- Butane lighter

Clothing
- Waterproof boots
- Wool socks
- Polypro liners
- Long underwear
- Long pants
- Sweater or sweatshirt
- Jacket
- Parka or poncho
- Gloves
- Cap/hat
- Wide brimmed hat
- Sunglasses

- Camp shoes or sandals

Personal/Toiletry/Misc.
- Toothbrush
- Shampoo/conditioner
- Safety razor
- Deodorant
- Moisturizer
- Soap
- Towel
- Toilet tissue
- First aid kit
- Medicines and vitamins
- Sunscreen and lip balm
- Insect repellent
- Whistle
- Flashlight and batteries
- Repair kit/sewing kit
- Watch
- Compass and maps
- Travel alarm clock

Documents
- Photocopies of all important documents
- Copies of prescriptions
- ATM/credit/debit card
- Traveler's checks
- Passport
- Travel visas
- Extra copies of passport photos
- Plane/train tickets
- Identification (student id, driver license, etc.)

Optional Items
- Nature guide
- Travel guide book
- Binoculars
- Hand warmers
- Ear plugs
- Book
- Camera
- Extra film or memory card

3 Season Backpacking Checklist

The following checklist will keep you prepared for backpacking throughout most of the year with the exception of winter.

- Backpack
- Tent- 3 or 4 season
- Tarp or ground cloth
- Sleeping bag
- Sleeping pad
- Stove
- Fuel (canisters or fuel bottles)
- Lighters
- Waterproof matches
- Cooking set
- Bowl/plate, mug, flatware
- Water bottles
- Flashlight or headlamp
- Extra batteries
- Knife or multi-tool
- Water filter or tablets
- First aid kit
- Repair kit
- Sunglasses
- Sunscreen/lip balm

- Nylon rope
- Map & compass

Clothing

Base Layer
- Light to medium long underwear top and bottoms
- Synthetic t-shirt
- Synthetic underwear
- Synthetic shorts

Outer Layer
- Fleece jacket or wool sweater
- Wind jacket
- Wind pants
- Waterproof jacket
- Waterproof pants
- Waterproof gaiters

Accessories
- Fleece or wool hat
- Fleece or wool gloves
- Bandana or handerkchief
- Hat or cap
- Waterproof hiking boots
- Fleece or wool socks (2-3 pairs)
- Synthetic sock liners (2 pairs)
- Camp shoes or sandals

Winter checklist

In addition, if you are planning to be traveling during the winter you should plan to add the following items:

- Snow tools (shovel, ice ax)
- Fleece jacket or wool sweater
- Down-fill jacket or synthetic-fill jacket
- Pile or fleece pants
- Wool or fleece hat
- Additional hat
- Wool or fleece gloves
- Shell mits (waterproof)
- Down booties
- Snow shoes or skis

Food and meals

If you are planning to prepare your own meals along the way, you will need to do some significant planning to make certain that you have food that will last during the trip and that will also provide you with adequate nutrition, especially considering the amount of physical activity that you are going to endure.

Breakfast Foods

Remember that it is never a good idea to try and skip breakfast. What you eat for breakfast sets the tone for the rest of the day and you need to make certain that you have plenty of energy. Some possible breakfast foods might include:

- Hot cereals-wheat, oat, corn, rice, grits, etc.
- Granola bar
- Fruit-think single items such as mixed fruit or raisins
- Fruit juice-choose pure fruit juice for the most nutrition, not fruit flavored drinks.
- Hot drinks-tea, cocoa, spiced hot cider, coffee

Lunch

Your noon meal should provide ample carbohydrates for plenty of energy. It should also focus on as little preparation time as possible. Some ideas include:

- Fortified crackers
- Cracker spreads-honey, jelly, peanut butter, etc.
- Tuna
- Beef Jerky
- Fruit
- Trail snacks
- Hot soup or some other hot dish such as baked beans
- Fruit drink

Dinner

Your evening meal should contain enough calories and protein while also being warm and filling. Some possible ideas include:

- A hot main dish-starch (noodles, rice, potatoes), sauce (gravies, meat broth) and a meat (ham, beef, chicken, etc.)
- Instant soup
- Instant potatoes
- Macaroni and cheese
- Instant rice
- Freeze dried or fresh vegetables
- Crackers
- Fruit drink
- Hot drink
- Dessert-pudding, fruit cup, etc.
- Condiments-sweetener, cream powder, milk powder, seasonings, flavored tea, instant hot soup, fruits, nuts, etc.

Backpacking Recipes

Easy Breakfast Casserole

Ingredients
- 1 ¾ cup instant mashed potatoes
- ½ cup freeze dried eggs
- 1 ½ cup water
- 1 tbsp powdered milk

Combine all of the powdered items in a zip lock freezer bag for easy traveling. While on the trail, heat water and add to bag and stir. Let sit for five minutes.

Banana and Peanut Butter Wrap

Ingredients
- 1 small banana
- Peanut butter
- 1 tortilla

Cut banana into slices. Spread peanut butter onto tortilla and place banana slices on PB. Roll and enjoy!

Tuna Salad Wrap

Ingredients
- Small package of tuna
- 1 packet mayo
- 1 packet relish
- 2 tortillas

Combine everything except tortilla, spread on tortilla and enjoy.

Conclusion

Hopefully this introductory guide will have provided you with some of the basic information that you need to make your first backpacking trip a success. Keep in mind that when you are on the trail you should always expect the unexpected, but with careful planning and research you should be able to minimize the risks so that you will be able to simply relax and have fun.

Backpacking is a wonderful hobby that can provide you not only with fun but also a wide array of experiences as you encounter people from around the world and learn about other cultures.

Each and every day that you are on the trail is an adventure!

Other books by Psylon Press:

100% Blonde Jokes
R. Cristi
ISBN 978-0-9866004-1-8

Choosing a Dog Breed Guide
Eric Nolah
ISBN 978-0-9866004-5-6

Best Pictures Of Paris
Christian Radulescu
ISBN 978-0-9866004-8-7

Best Gift Ideas For Women
Taylor Timms
ISBN 978-0-9866004-4-9

Top Bikini Pictures
Taylor Timms
ISBN 978-0-9866426-3-0

Cross Tattoos
Johnny Karp
ISBN 978-0-9866426-4-7

Beautiful Breasts Pictures
Taylor Timms
ISBN 978-1-926917-01-6

For more books please visit:
www.psylonpress.com

www.ingramcontent.com/pod-product-compliance
Lightning Source LLC
LaVergne TN
LVHW051850080426
835512LV00018B/3167